Nehemiah

–PRINCIPLES FOR LIFE

CWR

Selwyn Hughes
with Ian Sewter

Copyright © CWR 2005

Published 2005 by CWR, Waverley Abbey House, Waverley Lane, Farnham, Surrey GU9 8EP, England. Registered Charity No. 294387. Registered Limited Company No. 1990308. Reprinted 2009, 2010.

Text taken from *Every Day with Jesus, Rebuilding Broken Walls*, July/August 1995 by Selwyn Hughes. Adaptation and additional material by Ian Sewter.

The right of Selwyn Hughes and Ian Sewter to be identified as the authors of this work has been asserted by them in accordance with the Copyright, Designs and Patents Act 1988, sections 77 and 78.

See back of book for list of National Distributors.

Unless otherwise indicated, all Scripture references are from the Holy Bible: New International Version (NIV), copyright © 1973, 1978, 1984 by the International Bible Society.

Other Scripture quotations are marked:
The Message: Scripture taken from *The Message*. Copyright © 1993, 1994, 1995, 1996, 2000, 2001, 2002. Used by permission of NavPress Publishing Group.

Concept development, editing, design and production by CWR
Cover image: Roger Walker
Printed in Latvia by Yeomans Press

ISBN: 978-1-85345-335-9

Contents

Introduction

We embark now on what hopefully will turn out to be one of the most profitable spiritual voyages we have ever taken – a study of the book of Nehemiah. The main events of the book took place in the spring and summer of the year 445 BC. During this period Nehemiah made the journey from Susa, near the Persian Gulf, to the city of Jerusalem in order to restore the city's ruined defences. His story is regarded by many as one of the liveliest in the Bible. The late Dr Martyn Lloyd-Jones said: 'No one leaps out of the pages of the Old Testament and grabs your attention as does Nehemiah.' I agree.

As a young man I was told that whatever career I chose for myself, I would never be able to serve the Lord effectively until I understood the principles set out in the book of Nehemiah. I found that advice to be true. To enter into any career, whether in the business world or the Christian ministry, without an understanding of the spiritual principles that hold life together is utter foolishness. Many of these principles are illustrated most powerfully in the story of Nehemiah. I give you this promise – however effectively you may be serving the Lord now – the study of Nehemiah will help you serve Him better.

When we first meet Nehemiah he is serving as cupbearer (wine taster) in Susa, the principal palace and winter residence of the Persian kings. Nehemiah was a Jew, of course, probably of the tribe of Judah, but as cupbearer to the king he held a position of great eminence. As Nehemiah begins his story he tells of receiving a visit from his brother, Hanani, who reports that the gates and walls of Jerusalem are broken down. The Temple, rebuilt under Haggai and Zechariah, was still intact, but because of the decline in spirituality and general apathy, the city walls had been allowed to lie in ruins. In addition to this, marauders had burned down the gates and reduced them to a pile of ashes. Jerusalem, the city of God, was in a sorry state. Nehemiah's strong reaction to this news shows us where his real concerns lay: not in maintaining a good position in the Persian Empire but in achieving God's purposes for His holy city.

What, I wonder, is our reaction when we observe some of the modern 'walls' which God has inspired and instructed His people to build, that are now in a state of disrepair? Take, for example, the issue of marriage and family life. The walls that buttressed this most precious institution are in danger of being demolished. 'Marriages are a thing of the past,' says an article in one journal. 'Wedding rings are doomed.' How do we react when we see God's principles disregarded, His 'walls' being broken down? Do our personal concerns take priority over God's concerns? Nehemiah put first things first. So must we.

Nehemiah's intensely emotional reaction to the news concerning the plight of Jerusalem highlights the first of the many spiritual principles we shall discover in following his story: *before anyone can receive a blessing someone else has to be willing to bear a burden.* We can never lighten the load for others until we have first felt the weight of their troubles in our own soul. Nehemiah was not ready to put into action any kind of recovery plan for Jerusalem until he had first faced his feelings and wept because of its ruined state. Likewise, we are fit to do God's work only when we have faced matters and recognised how they are in reality – when we accept the truth about a situation. Look around you today and see things as they are, not as you would like them to be. Are you aware of any broken-down 'walls'? The walls of your devotional life perhaps. Your family. Your church. Is there something for which you should be grieving at this moment? A ruin you are not prepared to acknowledge?

Remember, you can't begin to rebuild a crumbling wall unless first you are willing to mourn over it.

As we consider how Nehemiah wept over the condition of Jerusalem it seems appropriate to remind ourselves that he wasn't the only person to weep over the holy city. Our Lord wept for the city too. Letting things affect us emotionally is not a sign of lack of faith in God, but we must not allow those matters to drag us down into self-pity. God's strength and resources are given to us not so that we can deny our feelings but to support us in them and bring us through.

The book of Nehemiah falls naturally into two parts. The first six chapters deal with the reconstruction of Jerusalem's walls; the last seven chapters with the re-instruction of the people. The theme however is the same throughout and can be summarised by a keyword: *restoration*. Nehemiah strove to restore the work of God and the people of God. Nehemiah is a 'type' of Christ because he relinquishes a privileged position to identify with his people, he fulfils his mission to restore people to God and he overcomes intense opposition by a life of prayer. Nehemiah could hardly be a better role model for us today as we seek to rebuild spiritual truth and restore our own neighbours and nation to God.

WEEK 1

Principles of Prayer

Opening Icebreaker

Choose an event, animal or object to describe your prayer life, eg: racing car – roaring on all cylinders; dodo – extinct; leap year – only happens once in a while; sunrise – every morning, etc.

Bible Reading

• Nehemiah 1:1–2:10

Opening Our Eyes

When we have a vision of spiritual ruin we are tempted to exclaim: 'We are helpless to do anything about it'. But what should we do after such moments of revelation? We should do what Nehemiah did – turn to fervent believing prayer. Look with me now at Nehemiah's prayer. Clearly, he was a man whose soul had been fed on the Word of God. His words were cast in the mould of God's revelation of Himself as given in the Scriptures – a characteristic of all great prayer warriors. He reminds the Almighty of His greatness and His awesomeness and the fact that He is a covenant-keeping God. He stands in both awe and adoration before Him, recognising His sovereignty. The greater God becomes to him, the smaller his problem appears in comparison. Nehemiah is then moved to confess the sins of his people and admits that their troubles stemmed from disobedience. Usually sin is the cause of our failures, and where there is sin it must always be confessed.

The attitude underlying Nehemiah's prayer is important to note: it is an attitude of reverence and submission. One person has said: 'The self-sufficient do not pray; they merely talk to themselves. The self-satisfied will not pray; they have no knowledge of their need. The self-righteous cannot pray; they have no basis on which to come to God'. When there is no reverence for God there will be few answers from God. In claiming the provision God made for His people, the godly Nehemiah reveals another great principle, namely that prayer must be based on the promises of God. 'Remember Your instructions to Moses,' he says, and then, paraphrasing the words the Lord gave to Moses, he claims the fulfilment of the promise. Nehemiah's confidence in the Lord as a promise-keeper is so great that he knows God will work out the details. Finally the prayer closes with a request that God will give him favour with the king of Persia – King Artaxerxes. Nehemiah knows it will be harder for him to leave the court than it was to enter it. He is a trusted and important man. But he accepts, too, that with God all things are possible.

Many commentators point out that the prayer pattern Nehemiah followed parallels the 'outline' of prayer which our Lord gave to His disciples in Luke 11. But prayer depends on more than just keeping to a pattern. It has been said: 'God does not hear our prayers so much as hear *us*' – in other words, what we put of ourselves into our prayers. Nehemiah continued entreating the Lord's favour for four months! (See Neh. 1:1 Kislev [November/ December] and Neh. 2:1 Nisan [March/April].) 'Persistence in prayer,' as the old saying goes, 'is what makes the difference.' Do we hear Nehemiah's kind of praying nowadays? Sadly, not as often as we ought. Most modern-day prayers are token prayers asking God to bless this, that and the other. Powerful praying flows out of seeing the situation as it is. And in seeing God as He is.

After four months the king eventually asks Nehemiah why he is sad. Nehemiah immediately demonstrates his reliance on God by sending off a prayer-o-gram before replying. Prayer-o-grams have their place, but they must never be seen as substitutes for fervent, believing intercession. We would all like to be able to pray Mini prayers and get Rolls-Royce blessings. But some rewards in prayer come only in proportion to the effort.

Discussion Starters

1. Why do we pray?

_____

_____

_____

_____

_____

2. How did Nehemiah's prayer reflect his attitude to God?

_____

_____

_____

_____

_____

3. Why did Nehemiah confess sins he had not personally committed?

_____

_____

_____

_____

_____

4. List the principles of effective prayer.

_____

_____

_____

_____

_____

5. What are your own experiences of prayer and how could you develop a deeper prayer life?

_____

_____

_____

_____

_____

6. What is the purpose and value of prayer-o-grams?

_____
_____
_____
_____
_____

7. Identify similarities and differences between Nehemiah's prayer and the Lord's Prayer.

_____
_____
_____
_____
_____

8. If God is a God of grace why does He reward persistent prayer?

_____
_____
_____
_____
_____

9. Why should we quote Scripture in our prayers?

_____
_____
_____
_____
_____

10. How has God answered some of your prayers?

_____
_____
_____
_____
_____

Personal Application

Prayer is a vital part of our relationship with God. It involves both listening and speaking to Him and will significantly determine our spiritual strength and effectiveness. We should therefore make every effort to learn and apply the principles of prayer in our own lives. *The Message* paraphrases Jesus' instruction to the sleeping disciples in Matthew 26:41, 'Stay alert; be in prayer so you don't wander into temptation without even knowing you're in danger. There is a part of you that is eager, ready for anything in God. But there's another part that's as lazy as an old dog sleeping by the fire.' All too easily we can allow our prayer lives to wither. Instead let us be disciplined and determined to be faithful in our prayer life. Remember too, that prayer is not just about petitions but about praise, thankfulness and joy (Phil. 4:4–7; Psa. 16:11).

Seeing Jesus in the Scriptures

Jesus was a man of prayer. He did nothing without first knowing His Father's will (John 5:19; Matt. 26:36–39). Jesus would rise early in the morning and often withdrew to lonely places to pray (Mark 1:35; Luke 5:16). Like Nehemiah, an intense period of prayer and fasting preceded His public ministry (Luke 4:1–15). Jesus still lives to intercede for us (Heb. 7:23–25) and it is because of Him that we can come before the throne of God to seek help in time of need (Heb. 4:14–16; 10:19–23).

WEEK 2

Principles of Leadership and Work

Opening Icebreaker

In your experience of school, sport, work, etc what are the characteristics of good leaders and good workers?

Bible Readings

- Nehemiah 2:11–18; 3:1–12

Opening Our Eyes

Management experts tell us one of the first principles of leadership is *co-ordination*. This involves blending people and their activities together in a way that successfully contributes to the whole. While the Church should not think of itself as a business affair, it ought nevertheless to be businesslike in all its affairs. Co-ordination is needed as greatly in the Church as it is in business. Those churches with the pastor-does-it-all approach will never develop properly. Such an attitude curbs the ministry which God has given to *every* believer. No co-ordination – no corporate or individual development and growth. It is as simple as that.

Another important principle of leadership is *co-operation*. Under God, Nehemiah brings together a powerful taskforce from different walks of life – priests, Levites, rulers, common people, merchants, temple servants, guards, farmers and goldsmiths. I heard one management expert say the word 'success' should be spelt 't-e-a-m-w-o-r-k'. His observation that 'if the whole prospers the individual will prosper' deserves emphasis. Notice how in the reconstruction of the Jeshanah Gate we read that repairs were carried out by men from Gibeon and Mizpah. These had little to gain themselves by fortifying Jerusalem as they lived some distance from the city. They could easily have allowed their own interests to draw them away from such personally unrewarding work. Yet God's purpose for Jerusalem was that its walls should be a symbol of salvation and its gates a symbol of praise. We can safely assume, I think, that though they lived some distance from Jerusalem it was a matter of great concern to them that these symbols of God's glory should be restored. The point has been made before – if we belong to Christ then all personal preoccupations and interests ought to be secondary to the building up of His kingdom. Nothing, *nothing* must take precedence over this.

A third principle of successful leadership is *commendation*. By this is meant a readiness to note and praise honest effort and to take a personal interest in those for whom one is responsible. Although in this third chapter we do not see Nehemiah actively going around praising people, we certainly see him taking a strong personal interest in his workers. Some might find the recital of the names of all the people who worked on the different gates somewhat tedious, but it reveals a lot about Nehemiah's *awareness* of who each person was, what they did and where they worked. For example, we are told that Hanun and the residents of Zanoah repaired 500 yards of broken-down wall (3.13), while next to them, Malkijah, working alone, repaired only the Dung Gate (3.14). Nehemiah, however, included both in the list of people commended, and did not allow the extent of one person's accomplishments to prevent him from recognising the efforts of another. In Nehemiah's eyes every person had the same worth and was not to be manipulated or exploited. Every one of us needs to feel that we count for something. I know I do, and I am sure you do also. God, of course, appreciates us. Scripture leaves us in no doubt about that. But it's nice to be appreciated by those with skin on also.

The last principle is *communication*. This involves the instruction of each worker so that he or she knows what to do and where to do it. It also involves the delegation of authority so that decisions do not need to be constantly referred to the top.

Discussion Starters

1. What made Nehemiah a good leader?

_____
_____
_____
_____

2. Why is commendation of people important? Is your tendency to commend or criticise people?

_____
_____
_____
_____

3. Why should we become involved in activities that do not directly benefit us?

_____
_____
_____
_____

4. How could you contribute more effectively in a team of which you are a member?

_____
_____
_____
_____

5. What qualities do you see in other members of your group?

_____
_____
_____
_____

6. List different roles that exist within the Body of Christ. Can you match a role to each member of your group?

_____

_____

_____

_____

_____

7. Why do some people not take part in church activities and how could they be encouraged to participate?

_____

_____

_____

_____

_____

8. Is communication in your church effective? How could it be improved?

_____

_____

_____

_____

_____

9. What training would help individuals and the Church in general to be more effective?

_____

_____

_____

_____

_____

Personal Application

We are all members of the Body of Christ and have a vital part to play (1 Cor. 12). If you are unsure of your own role in helping to build and restore then seek God and wise people to give you a sense of direction and purpose. 'For we are God's workmanship, created in Christ Jesus to do good works, which God prepared in advance for us to do' (Eph. 2:10). Why not use CWR's *Discovering Your Basic Gift* questionnaire.[1]

Sometimes with spiritual matters our view becomes clouded by familiarity and we need someone with a clearer spiritual perspective to confront us and say: 'This is not the way things should be'. How about you? Look around you right now. I ask you again: Are there 'walls' in your life lying flat that should be standing? Perhaps once you were on fire for God but now you rationalise your Christian experience and comment: 'Life nowadays is tough. I can't be expected to be on top of things all the time'. Dangerous thinking.

Permit me to come alongside you right now and say: 'Take a look around. See the walls that are lying flat? That is not what God wants. Ruined walls do not glorify God. *Come, let us rebuild*'. I am discovering some 'walls' in my own life that need rebuilding. I wonder, is it the same with you? If so, let's begin rebuilding – and without delay.

Seeing Jesus in the Scriptures

Jesus, like Nehemiah, took a motley collection of people from diverse backgrounds and built them into an enthusiastic and committed team which 'turned the world upside down'.

---

[1] This can be obtained from CWR or downloaded free from www.cover2cover.org

WEEK 3

Overcoming Opposition

Opening Icebreaker

'Sticks and stones may break my bones but words can never harm me.' Discuss how true this proverb is.

Bible Readings

- Nehemiah 2:10; 19–20; 4:1–23; 6:17–19

Opening Our Eyes

When Sanballat, the governor of Samaria, and Tobiah his associate knew that Nehemiah was on his way to Jerusalem they were extremely displeased. They were men of influence and power who opposed and tried to outmanoeuvre Nehemiah in everything he did. Sanballat and Tobiah knew perfectly well what Nehemiah was after – the restoration of the holy city. And being enemies of God they would focus their hatred not only on the Lord but on His servant also.

Sanballat, Tobiah and Geshem know that weak, demoralised people are inclined to give way when threatened. But they reckon without Nehemiah! Before the Jews have time to react to their threats, Nehemiah makes his reply: 'The God of heaven will give us success,' he says. 'We his servants will start rebuilding.' Then, addressing the evil triumvirate, he adds: 'but as for you, you have no share in Jerusalem or any claim or historic right to it' (2:20). How desperately we need men and women like this in the Church today; people who will stand up to the devil and say: 'Make all the threats you like. We will not be diverted from our purpose of building walls in God's kingdom and bringing praise and glory to our King.' Nehemiah's confidence was not in his mandate from King Artaxerxes but in his commission from the King of heaven. This is why he is able to stand up to the enemies of God and say in effect: 'I am standing on God's territory – and you have no right to be anywhere near it.' Satan is camped on much of God's property nowadays. It's time to say to him: 'In the name of Jesus get out'.

Later we read that Sanballat and Tobiah use the weapons of ridicule and sarcasm to discourage the workers and then plot to fight and stir up trouble. Nehemiah, when faced with criticism, took the route every one of us should take when confronted with the same problem –

he poured out his heart to God in prayer. But this time the situation demands not only prayer but action. 'But we prayed to our God,' he says, '*and* posted a guard' (4:9, my italics). There are times when prayer is enough to deal with a situation, but there are other times when prayer needs to be accompanied by action. Faith must join hands with works.

Though morale was high, the moment came, however, when due to the threats from Sanballat and the others, some of the people in Judah became discouraged and wanted to quit. They said the reason for their discouragement was physical exhaustion, but Nehemiah knew the real reason was fear. This is why he turned their attention to the Lord who is 'great and awesome' (4:14). Fear can only be overcome with faith; not faith in oneself but faith in God. Is fear knocking at your door right now? Then, as you answer its knock, take Jesus with you. Don't be surprised if you find no one there.

Nehemiah's three-pronged counter-attack – prayer, vigilant guards and the charge to look continually to the Lord – is so successful that he is able to write: 'We all returned to the wall, each to his own work' (4:15). Half of the workforce stand on guard while the other half work. A trumpeter is ready to summon everyone in the event of a surprise attack. 'Those who carried materials' we read, 'did their work with one hand and held a weapon in the other' (v.17).

Discussion Starters

1. Why do Christians experience opposition to their faith and work?

_____

_____

_____

_____

_____

2. What types of opposition do we face?

_____

_____

_____

_____

3. How should we overcome opposition?

_____

_____

_____

_____

4. Why is prayer sometimes insufficient to overcome opposition?

_____

_____

_____

_____

_____

5. Are you currently experiencing any opposition to your faith and how is that affecting you?

_____

_____

_____

_____

6. What spiritual weapons has God provided for us and how should they be used?

_____

_____

_____

_____

_____

7. Why did the people from Judah use the excuse of exhaustion when they were really afraid?

_____

_____

_____

_____

_____

8. How can we help each other overcome opposition?

_____

_____

_____

_____

_____

9. What helps us overcome opposition (1 John 4:18; 5:4)?

_____

_____

_____

_____

_____

Personal Application

As we seek to rebuild the walls that have been broken down either by neglect or by Satan and his forces, let us not forget that we are engaged in a battle as well as in a building programme. Scripture says that, 'the devil prowls around like a roaring lion looking for someone to devour' (1 Pet. 5:8). And again: 'For our struggle is not against flesh and blood, but against the rulers, against the authorities, against the powers of this dark world' (Eph. 6:12). We must go about our task with a sword in one hand and a trowel in the other. In addition to the gifts God has given us to build His kingdom in this world, we need a sword to defend ourselves against Satan and his forces. The sword of the Spirit is the Word of God, and the more we memorise the Word and meditate on it, the stronger will be our resistance to the devil and his armies. We must be careful, however, that battling does not replace building. One must not be done at the expense of the other. The walls have to go up – no matter what.

Seeing Jesus in the Scriptures

'Let us fix our eyes on Jesus, the author and perfecter of our faith, who for the joy set before him endured the cross, scorning its shame, and sat down at the right hand of the throne of God. Consider him who endured such opposition from sinful men, so that you will not grow weary and lose heart.' Hebrews 12:2–3

WEEK 4

The Fear of the Lord and a Godly Lifestyle

Opening Icebreaker

Describe the perfect Christian leader in terms of character and lifestyle (not abilities).

Bible Readings

- Nehemiah 5:1–19
- Proverbs 9:10

Opening Our Eyes

In this chapter the perspective suddenly changes. Israel's enemies and the rebuilding of Jerusalem's walls take second place to a more immediate and pressing problem – internal dissension. The people were upset because of a food crisis – a famine – the effects of which were made worse by the increased number of Jews in Jerusalem. The problem was further exacerbated by heavy taxation and exploitation of the poor by wealthy and unscrupulous leaders. Nehemiah knew that what was being practised by the loan sharks went completely against the instructions God had given and so he courageously confronts them. He reproaches the leaders for the fact that they have sold their own people into slavery, and they are shamed into silence when he goes on to say that the people they sold to the Gentiles have been bought back by Nehemiah and his friends. He challenges them to return the land, property and interest they had taken immediately.

Nehemiah exhorts the leaders to 'walk in the fear of our God' (v.9). But to instruct those responsible to 'Do as I say' would have resulted in disastrous consequences if his own conduct had not been above reproach. Nehemiah tells us that though he held an eminent position in Judah, he never used that position to serve his own interests. He says, '… out of reverence for God I did not act like that' (v.15). In these words we discover the dynamic that motivated the godly Nehemiah: *reverence for God.* Unless you and I, as Christian people, revere God, we are not going to progress very far along the spiritual path. Reverence for the Lord is described in Scripture as the foundation of right conduct (Psa. 111:10; Prov. 1:7). Underlying 'reverence for God' or, as some translations put it, 'the fear of the Lord', is *holiness.* No one can ascend the hill of the Lord, unless he has clean hands and a pure heart (Psa. 24:3–4). And 'without holiness no-one will see the Lord' (Heb. 12:14).

What is holiness? 'The secret of success in the Christian life,' I was once told by an old and godly pastor, 'is not just saying "No" to whatever is wrong, but saying "Yes" to what is right.' Nehemiah not only said 'No' to wrongdoing, but 'Yes' to God's plans. 'I devoted myself to the work on this wall,' he tells us (5:16). More is required of us as Christians than turning our backs on that which is negative; we must also turn our faces towards the positive – the will and purpose of God. Nehemiah's decision to devote himself to rebuilding the wall instead of developing an affluent lifestyle shows him to have been purposeful and committed to one task. He did not get caught up with private ventures or peripheral issues with their distractions. Instead he concentrated on one thing only. The charge of pursuing conflicting interests could not be laid at his door. Even his servants worked shoulder to shoulder with the rest of the people.

From Nehemiah's example another important principle emerges: *single-mindedness*. Whatever we are called to do for God, we will not experience success unless we are single-minded. It is so easy to allow ourselves to be sidetracked by some other 'worthy' cause and get caught up in pursuing things that, though good in themselves, prevent us from giving all our energies to the one thing we are called to do. Sometimes the good has to be disregarded in order to achieve the best.

Discussion Starters

1. Why is 'the fear [reverence] of the Lord the foundation of wisdom'?

_____

_____

_____

_____

2. Why is the 'fear of the Lord' different to being afraid of God?

_____

_____

_____

_____

3. Define holiness and how it may be developed in our lives.

_____

_____

_____

_____

4. If God is a God of grace and forgives sin why is holiness so important?

_____

_____

_____

_____

_____

5. How are people exploited today in our country and throughout the world and how could we help?

_____

_____

_____

_____

6. Why may God's leaders exploit God's people and how could that be avoided?

_____

_____

_____

_____

7. How did Nehemiah handle his anger and what lessons can we learn for our own lives?

_____

_____

_____

_____

_____

8. Is it difficult to be single-minded for God in today's world?

_____

_____

_____

_____

_____

9. Why do people find it difficult to speak out against wrong-doing?

_____

_____

_____

_____

_____

10. Why may internal dissension be more dangerous than external opposition to the work of God?

_____

_____

_____

_____

Personal Application

In an age when standards are being lowered and moral absolutes ignored, it is so easy to rationalise issues and cut corners morally on the basis that everyone else is doing the same. But blessed are those who, like Nehemiah, stand up for truth and righteousness and say: 'But out of reverence for God I did not act like that.' From this incident we also learn that sometimes more is needed than just to think through issues in an objective way; we also need courage to face and confront those with whom we strongly disagree. Many of us, whenever we know we are right about an issue (at least in our own eyes), are content to settle for being right. Only under extreme provocation do we discuss the cause of our anger or concern with the offending party. It is all too easy to find reasons for not doing what we know needs to be done. The fear of people can sometimes be a snare that traps us (Prov. 29:25) and overcomes our fear of the Lord. We need, like Nehemiah, to boldly speak out against things that are wrong and hindering the work of God.

Seeing Jesus in the Scriptures

Jesus did not exploit His disciples but rather acted as their servant when He washed their feet (John 13:1–17) and gave His life as a ransom for many (Mark 10:45). Due to His reverence for God Jesus submitted His own will to God's will and single-mindedly finished the work that He was given to do (Luke 22:42; John 17:4; 19:30).

WEEK 5

Back to the Bible

Opening Icebreaker

Test your knowledge of the Bible. Take it in turns to name a book of the Bible and try to remember all 66. The winner can read the first passage in the readings!

Bible Readings

- Nehemiah 8:1–18
- Matthew 7:24–27
- James 1:22–25

Opening Our Eyes

Once the great task of the rebuilding of the wall and the census has been completed, Nehemiah fades into the background for a while and Ezra the scribe comes into the spotlight. He had been sent to Jerusalem some 13 years earlier to rebuild the Temple, but now comes forward when asked to read from the Scripture. It is the seventh month, the most solemn month of the year, ushered in by the Feast of Trumpets. So universal is the spiritual awakening that the people leave their towns and make their way to Jerusalem 'as one man' to hear Ezra read the Scriptures to them. As soon as Ezra opened up the Book of the Law and praised the Lord, all the people stood up, lifted up their hands to heaven and said 'Amen!', which, as you know, means 'So be it'. 'Then they bowed down and worshipped the LORD with their faces to the ground' (8:6). This was not, as some suggest, the practice of bibliolatry – the worship of a book. The praise and adoration was for God and in anticipation of what they were to hear from His Word.

The point we need to get hold of is this: it is not enough to hear the Word of God; it must also be carefully explained and then put into practice. That is why God has gifted certain people in the Church to explain the Scriptures. When the great nineteenth-century Baptist preacher C.H. Spurgeon first came to London he noticed that the people who attended his church were so starved spiritually that even a morsel of biblical exposition was a treat to them. By the time he completed his ministry it was said that his people knew more of the Bible than many a theologian. Today churches tend to emphasise experience rather than Bible exposition. People languish where the Word of God is not explained. However spiritually exciting or dramatic things might appear, it is not a true movement of the Spirit unless it touches and affects our wills. The spiritual renewal described in this chapter began with the people's expectation, developed through the exposition of the Word, and moved on to touch the emotions. Finally it motivated their will to put God's instructions into their experience.

The spiritual movement that began in the five- or six-hour meeting culminates in the people desiring to know and *do* the will of the Lord. The next day following what might be described as 'the day of renewal', the heads of the families meet with Ezra for more instruction from the Word. They find they have not kept the Feast of Tabernacles which, according to the instructions God gave to Moses, should take place during the seventh month. The Feast commemorated the Exodus and reminded the Jews of the wandering of their fathers in the desert, when God made the people 'live in booths' (shelters of branches – Lev. 23:43). Once the heads of the families realise their oversight, they determine to remedy the situation immediately. Their decision to keep the feast reveals their willingness to submit to the Word of God and do as it commands – not just to hear it. So great is their longing to know more of God's Word that Ezra is asked to hold *daily* Bible studies. One day of teaching is not enough for these people – they want instruction on a regular basis. With such spiritual hunger, is it any wonder revival is in the air?

Discussion Starters

1. How did the people respond when they heard the Word of God?

_____

_____

_____

_____

_____

2. How important is regular Bible reading?

_____

_____

_____

_____

_____

3. Why may those who read the Bible be deceived?

_____

_____

_____

_____

_____

4. Which Bible reading aids have you found helpful to explain the Scriptures?

_____

_____

_____

_____

_____

5. What is your favourite Bible passage and why?

_____

_____

_____

_____

_____

6. Should reading the Bible ever cause us to weep?

_____

_____

_____

_____

7. Compare the Bible to great works of literature. What are the similarities and differences?

_____

_____

_____

_____

_____

8. How can we present Bible truths to a modern (non-book) culture?

_____

_____

_____

_____

_____

9. Recount an occasion when God has spoken to you very clearly through the Bible.

_____

_____

_____

_____

_____

10. Are there any areas of weakness in your Bible knowledge and how could these be strengthened?

_____

_____

_____

_____

_____

Personal Application

It is interesting to read that the Israelites had not kept the Feast of Tabernacles since the days of Joshua – a period of around 1,000 years. Imagine that! God had given specific instructions to His people so they would ever remember His goodness in delivering them from slavery in Egypt (Lev. 23:33–44). They neglected to obey God's Word and ended up neglecting God Himself. When we neglect to read and follow the truths of the Bible we drift into a position where we neglect its author and our spirituality crumbles like the walls of Jerusalem or the house built on sand. The Bible was never given to us as an occasional reference book for our dusty bookshelves but as a manufacturers handbook and spiritual nourishment for our daily lives. We were never meant to live by food alone but by reading and living by every word that comes from God (Matt. 4:4).

Seeing Jesus in the Scriptures

Jesus Himself often referred to the Scriptures. He quoted them to overcome the devil when He was tempted and regularly used them in His preaching and teaching (eg, from the Gospel of Luke 4:1–21; 6:1–5; 7:27; 8:10; 14:35; 18:18–20; 19:46; 20:37, 41–43; 22:37). Jesus did not come to replace the Scriptures but to fulfil them (Matt. 5:17). If the Son of God relied so much on the Word of God then we too should seek to read, understand, apply and share the truths of the Bible in our own lives.

WEEK 6

Principles of a Good Confession

Opening Icebreaker

Ask people in the group to briefly share about a time when God has blessed them.

Bible Readings

- Nehemiah 9:1–36
- Psalm 32:1–5
- 1 John 1:9
- 1 Timothy 6:12–14

Opening Our Eyes

We now see the people going without food, dressed in sackcloth and with dust on their heads. What has gone wrong? Has some awful sin been uncovered? No, they are giving evidence of their contrition. Their fasting bears witness to their devotion, the sackcloth symbolises their inner repentance, and the dust on their heads is the external sign of the sorrow they feel in their hearts. Their prayer begins, as do all great prayers, with worship, adoration and praise by acknowledging that God alone created heaven and earth and all living things.

The corporate prayer of repentance offered by the Jews has only one petition: that God will have mercy and not think lightly of their hardships. But first they remind God that He is a covenant-keeping God, and they acknowledge that He has always acted justly and been faithful to them. Next they confess their sin to Him in the words 'we did wrong' (9:33). I once heard a famous American preacher claim that, 'the three hardest words to say in all the world are "I was wrong"'. Yet here the Jewish people are saying just that: 'we were wrong'. One thing that strikes me about this whole prayer is the absence of excuses. True repentance always involves an admission of wrongdoing – without excuses. If we try to excuse ourselves by saying, 'Lord, I know I was wrong in doing this, but I was a little unbalanced at the time because of all the pressures on me,' we are not truly repenting. Repentance offers no excuses, indulges in no prevarications or rationalisations.

But much of the focus of the prayer of confession is not on the sinfulness of the people but the marvellous mercy and forgiving grace of God. Where sin abounds, grace super-abounds. Though Israel rebelled time and time again, the Lord stood by His people. Even when they made a golden calf and worshipped it He did not desert them (v.18), but continued to guide and protect them and provide everything they needed. Look at the way in which the words 'You' and 'they' are set against each other in describing the faithfulness of God and the stubbornness and recalcitrance of the people. God is faithful; the people unfaithful. God is consistent; the people are inconsistent. God is reliable; the people unreliable. As the Jews listen to this powerful prayer and the contrasts it presents, they have occasion to reflect on how much more faithful God is to His people than they are to Him. Who could blame Him if He abandoned us? But how wonderful it is that He does not. The confession and acknowledgement of God's goodness continues by considering the time when the Israelites first settled in Canaan – the period of the judges – and the monarchy. This review of their national history provides every one of the Jews listening with encouraging evidences of what God has done in the past, the awesome consequences of ingratitude and the inevitability of punishment if sin is not confessed. But most important of all, there is hope for the future. And that hope is based on the unchanging character of God. They see in the present a product of the past and the seed of the future. Their anticipation now is that the knowledge of past events will help them avoid the evil and follow the good. Their conviction is that a merciful God will once again forgive them and help them in their hour of need.

Discussion Starters

1. Should we still practise fasting today when confessing our sins and seeking God?

_____

_____

_____

_____

2. How did the psalmist feel before he confessed his sin?

_____

_____

_____

_____

_____

3. Why are we often reluctant to confess our sins?

_____

_____

_____

_____

_____

4. Should we confess our sins to church leaders or other believers?

_____

_____

_____

_____

_____

5. What is the nature of true confession and repentance of sin?

_____

_____

_____

_____

_____

6. Why should we reflect on the past?

_____

_____

_____

_____

_____

7. What caused the Israelites to forsake God time and time again?

_____

_____

_____

_____

_____

8. Why did God not abandon the Israelites?

_____

_____

_____

_____

_____

9. What is the benefit of confessing the truth of what Scripture says about God and ourselves?

_____

_____

_____

_____

_____

10. Why can we have hope for the future no matter what our past has been?

_____

_____

_____

_____

_____

Personal Application

We live in a day when people are quick to excuse themselves for their unacceptable behaviour by pleading: 'I've been hurt too so you can't expect me to behave properly under such circumstances. It's my parents' fault because they gave me a negative self-image. You can't blame me for the way I act.' Whatever you do, don't adopt this attitude when you come to God. Every one of us is culpable before Him. We have sinned because we like sinning. We have hurt Him because we wanted to hurt Him. So let there be no excuses when we seek forgiveness from Him. Say those three little words – 'I was wrong' – and cleansing will come hard on the heels of your confession. Then, like the psalmist, we will be able to say, 'Blessed is he whose transgressions are forgiven'. Instead of guilt and condemnation there will be peace and joy.

But remember that good confession also includes speaking out that which is true about God and His provisions for us. There is great power in speaking out the truths of Scripture; that we are loved by God, cleansed of sin, purified from shame, accepted in the beloved as His child and a joint heir with Christ. Particularly when we are tempted to despair or doubt let us turn to the Scriptures and confess the truth of God's love that will shine light into our darkness and stir our faith to flame once again.

Seeing Jesus in the Scriptures

'… Christ Jesus, who while testifying before Pontius Pilate made the good confession …' (1 Timothy 6:13).

WEEK 7

Covenant Commitment

Opening Icebreaker

Take it in turns to identify key elements of a marriage ceremony.

Bible Readings

- Nehemiah 9:38; 10:28–39
- Jeremiah 31:3–4, 33–34
- Matthew 26:26–28

Opening Our Eyes

The importance of making a binding agreement that commits oneself to a deeper relationship with God is something every one of us ought to understand and, whenever necessary, put into operation. Whatever words we use to describe it – dedication, consecration, covenant – the decision to commit oneself following confession of sin or when new challenges are being opened up by the Lord is an essential aspect of effective Christian living. Clearly, as a result of the exposition of Scripture and the powerful prayer of confession, the people under the leadership of Ezra and Nehemiah decided to conserve the spiritual gains by entering into a covenant (or agreement) with their covenant-keeping God. They solemnly commit themselves to following God and obeying His Word.

The final terms of the covenant sealed by the people have to do with maintaining the Temple and those who minister in it. This implies that God's house is once again central to the Jews' thinking. The commitment involves an assurance that there will be an adequate supply of wood, that the first fruits of the produce will be brought annually to the Lord, that tithes will be given, and so on. The people are, in other words, agreeing that the Lord's claim on their lives will touch everything they have and own – children, cattle, produce, even the new wine and oil. Whether Ezra drafted the covenant on his own or with the help of others we cannot be sure, but clearly great care was taken to cover every area of their lives. And with great solemnity the people commit themselves to maintaining the house of God. The commitment to ensuring that the things which had to do with the Temple were not neglected, though last in order, is not to be regarded as least in importance. There is always a strong link between spirituality and social conduct (though this is denied by some), and unless the worship of God (as represented by the house of God) is central, all kinds of social problems will arise. Without a strong base for worship neither the Church nor society can expect to survive.

The book of Nehemiah concludes by naming the priests, leaders and key workers involved in the restoration of Jerusalem followed by the joyful dedication of the new wall (Neh. 12:27). Eventually, Nehemiah went back to Babylon to serve King Artaxerxes but later returned to Jerusalem to ensure the people continued to follow the Lord. He found that God's people had once again begun to drift from the terms of their covenant commitment (Neh. 13:6ff). Nehemiah rebukes those in the wrong and exhorts the people to turn back to God.

How do we summarise what we learn from the life of this great and godly man? Without strong and capable spiritual leadership the people of God are like sheep without a shepherd. Moral and spiritual decline then soon sets in. To counteract this we must return to the Word of God, submit ourselves to it, confess our failures and our shortcomings and begin once again to delight in obeying the commandments of the Lord. Only then can we expect to be a people who reflect the glory of the Lord. Inevitably this passage causes us to remember our great covenant with God through Jesus Christ who is the mediator of a better covenant (Heb. 8:6). In this new covenant God promises to forgive our sins and enter into intimate relationship with each one of us.

Discussion Starters

1. What are the essential elements of a covenant?

_____

_____

_____

_____

_____

2. What did the Israelites commit themselves to do and how may this relate to us?

_____

_____

_____

_____

_____

3. Why did the Israelites drift from their covenant commitments and how can we avoid doing the same?

_____

_____

_____

_____

_____

4. How might we 'neglect the house of God'?

_____

_____

_____

_____

_____

5. What does communion mean to you?

_____

_____

_____

_____

_____

6. How should Christians regard the Sabbath or day of rest in our modern culture?

_____

_____

_____

_____

_____

7. Should Christians tithe (give a tenth of their income to the Lord)?

_____

_____

_____

_____

_____

8. In what sense is Nehemiah a 'type of Christ' (ie, what are the similarities between Nehemiah and Christ)?

_____

_____

_____

_____

_____

9. What are the main lessons you have learned from our studies in Nehemiah?

_____

_____

_____

_____

_____

Personal Application

The first point of the covenant instituted by Nehemiah is the need to submit to the authority of God's laws given in the Scriptures. The people know they cannot expect God's blessing without being obedient to Him. They also realise they have to act responsibly before Him, and that to pray and expect God's blessing and then go one's own way just will not work. Their history proves this. From this general commitment the people go on to make more specific ones. First, they agree to abstain from inter-marriage, commit themselves to keeping the Sabbath, and every seventh year let the ground lie fallow and cancel all debts.

Note the attention to detail in this covenant. Not one matter is left unidentified. Let us remember that when we commit ourselves to obeying the commandments of the Lord we must commit ourselves to obeying *all* the commandments of the Lord. 'Some' or 'most' is not enough. Israel's covenant with the Lord contains important principles for the Church here in the twenty-first century. Let us yield to His will and allow Him to develop within us a love for His Word, a deep desire to do His work and to minister to those who, in Christ's name, minister to us.

Seeing Jesus in the Scriptures

Jesus, like Nehemiah, has led us into a new relationship with God through a binding covenant. Every time we take communion we remember that through His death our sins are forgiven and that God has committed Himself to us, just as we have committed ourselves to follow Him.

Leader's Notes

Week 1: Principles of Prayer

Opening Icebreaker
The icebreaker should help people share and identify
their own experience of prayer in a non-threatening way.
You could prepare a list of other examples for people to
choose eg, yo-yo – up and down.

Bible Readings
This section is both the introduction to the book and
forms the basis of our first session on the subject of
prayer. It may also be helpful to read Luke 11:1–4 prior to
looking at the discussion points.

Aim of the Session
The aim of this session is to heighten our understanding
of the principles of prayer and motivate us to experience
a deeper and more fruitful prayer life. One of the most
important lessons we can learn is of patience and
persistence in prayer. As chapter 2 opens it has been four
months since Nehemiah first heard the news concerning
Jerusalem, during which time he has wept, mourned, fasted,
and prayed. Nehemiah did not dash impetuously to the task
the moment the need to rebuild Jerusalem's walls was made
apparent to him. He knew that to be successful in the work
he wanted to do for God he must have not only the favour
of the king but also God's blessing and direction.

This is one of the reasons we pray, for without God's
help we cannot achieve anything of eternal significance
(John 15:5). If we are too busy to pray then we are
busier than God intended us to be and we are relying
too much on our own resources. Notice that Nehemiah
did not speak to the king; the king spoke to him. How

important is timing in all that we seek to do for God.
Many a life has been shipwrecked spiritually because of
impulsiveness and haste. I know people who could have
been in a great ministry today but they failed the waiting
test. They sensed a need, and did not wait for God's
perfect timing in the matter. A right action can turn out to
be wrong simply because it was mistimed. God's timing is
always perfect. Ours is not.

The issue of Nehemiah confessing sins he had not
personally committed is an interesting one and is echoed
elsewhere in Scripture by such people as Daniel (Dan.
9:1–20). This practice reflects the ministry of a priest as
an intercessor who so closely identifies with sinful people
that he confesses their sins. On the day of atonement
the high priest confessed the 'wickedness and rebellion
of the Israelites – all their sins' (Lev. 16:21). Daniel, like
Nehemiah, was a faithful and obedient servant of God
and yet he confessed, '*our* unfaithfulness to you ... *we*
have sinned against you ... *we* have rebelled against him
... *we* have not obeyed' and 'confessing my sin and the
sin of *my* people' (Dan. 9:8–10,20, my italics). Of course
the ultimate example of such an intercessor is Jesus who,
although without sin Himself, 'bore our sins' (2 Cor.
5:18–21; 1 Pet. 2:24). If we are to intercede effectively for
God to move in our own nation then perhaps there are
times when we should pray for God to forgive *us*, and
not distance ourselves by asking God to forgive *them*.

Prayer is not a means of twisting God's arm or of earning
sufficient points to make Him act on our behalf and yet
'he rewards those who earnestly seek him' (Heb. 11:6).
Sometimes God blesses both good and evil people with
His provisions such as sunshine and rain even without
prayer, simply because He loves us and acts through
grace (Matt. 5:45). At other times we specifically need to
pray for rain (James 5:18). We should not take God or His
blessings for granted.

Week 2: Principles of Leadership and Work

Opening Icebreaker
Ask each person to share briefly, without stirring up past injustices committed by poor leaders!

Bible Readings
You may like to extend this session by also looking at passages about spiritual gifts given below.

Aim of the Session
We must remind ourselves of an important principle – that failure to understand and develop one's role in Christ's Body results in one's service for Christ becoming a hit-or-miss affair. The churches which are forging ahead and reaching out into their communities have leaders who understand this principle and help their people discover and develop their gifts. It is vital therefore that our churches are led by godly and wise leaders who train, motivate and place their members in roles that match their abilities and maximise their effectiveness. Have the people in your group discovered yet where they belong in Christ's Body? I believe that every Christian has at least one spiritual gift and that if that gift is not discovered and developed then the person can soon fall prey to discouragement and disillusionment – perhaps even despair. We don't drift into spiritual maturity; we develop it through prayer, desire and discipleship.

It may be appropriate to take extra time on this session and look at a list of God-given abilities in Romans 12:1–8, 1 Corinthians 12 and Ephesians 4:11. In addition we should consider each person's skills, desires, personality and life experiences. All of these factors combined with prayer, encouragement, training and opportunity will help each individual find a significant role in Christ's Body. The passage of 1 Corinthians 12:22–24 explains that the unseen parts of a body (such as heart, liver, lungs, kidneys, etc) are as important as the visible parts. We may not preach a sermon in a church service but making cups of tea, dealing with the collection, helping in Sunday School or typing the church newsletter are all vital roles in the life of a church. It has been suggested that the average person has more than 500 skills! Perhaps members of the group could list some of their abilities, passions and experiences to share with the group for prayer and discussion. For example, a car driver who enjoys talking to people and has a caring attitude might develop a ministry of visiting sick or elderly people. A couple in my own church whose baby died within a few days of being born have been used to speak to others who have suffered a similar experience. God knows that every individual is unique and He can lead us into a role that is just right for each one of us.

One of the key concepts of the Christian faith mentioned above is *discipleship*. A disciple is a person who is under training and development. Christ Himself chose disciples who He could train to become effective ministers of the gospel in word and deed. God has called us to be participators not spectators. Part of the responsibility of mature Christians is that they should actively seek to help, mentor and encourage others to develop their abilities and use them for the glory of God (Matt. 28:19–20). Part of the responsibility of every believer is to love God and actively seek to serve Him wherever they find themselves (Deut. 10:12). Churches need to teach and embody these concepts. Of course we also need to remind ourselves that a Christian teacher may serve God through their employment at school, whilst a Christian housewife serves God by caring for her family. Whatever we do we should 'work at it with all our heart, as working for the Lord, not for men' (Col. 3:23; see also Eph. 6:5–8).

Week 3: Overcoming Opposition

Opening Icebreaker
Some people are afraid of physical violence but we
should never underestimate the power of words alone.
Sarcasm, criticism and threats can be sufficient to deflect
us from good and godly goals (Prov. 12:18; Psa. 64:1–4).

Bible Readings
You may also like to read Ephesians 6:10–18 and
2 Corinthians 10:3–5 which refer to our spiritual weapons.
The record of Jesus' temptation is also helpful in showing
how He overcame opposition (Luke 4:1–13).

Aim of the Session
Sarcasm, derision and invective are some of Satan's chief
weapons when attempting to discourage God's people.
I have even known continued sarcasm to cause men
to leave the Christian ministry and return to secular
employment. Many Christians today will receive some
carping remark about their faith from colleagues or perhaps
from their own family. Satan can use even our loved ones
to discourage us. C.S. Lewis said in *God in the Dock*: 'It's
extraordinary how inconvenient it is to your family when
you get up early to go to church. It doesn't matter so much
if you get up early for anything else but if you get up
early for church it's selfish of you, you upset the home'.
Some Christians think God should preserve us from such
discouragement. However, His way is not to save us from
it, but to save us in it. Only when we learn to accept this
fact will we be unbeatable and unbreakable.

One thing becomes apparent from a study of Christian
history and it is this: whenever anyone says, 'Let us arise
and build,' Satan and his forces respond: 'Let us arise and
stop him'. About 50,000 Jews were living in Judah but
there appeared to be little concern among them about the
state of Jerusalem's walls and the ruined testimony of their

Jewish faith. Once it was known, however, that Nehemiah was on his way to rebuild Jerusalem, war was declared in the heavens. No battle can commence anywhere, in the spiritual sense, until somebody decides to stand up and challenge the things that need challenging. One thing is sure – when we stand up and are counted as citizens of the kingdom then Satan will throw all his weight against us.

I have seen many believers lulled by Satan into thinking that their long experience in the faith and understanding of Christian doctrine were all they needed to protect them from attack, but they found to their cost that this was insufficient. Spiritual opposition is not overcome by *our* experience or *our* understanding but can only be overcome by the spiritual armour and weapons that God has given us. Although not the place for a full exposition of this subject we particularly need to protect our mind from destructive thoughts and our heart from negative emotions. Remember how these influences prevented the Israelites from entering the promised land (Num. 13:25–14:4).

Paul, in listing the six main pieces of a soldier's equipment, does so in order to illustrate the six main ways we can defend ourselves against the power of Satan – truth, righteousness, steadfastness, faith, salvation and the Word of God. We can encourage and pray for each other when attacked but above all else, every believer has a personal responsibility to put on their own armour. When Jesus was in the wilderness He resisted every one of Satan's temptations by using the precise words of Scripture. He did not merely re-state a scriptural principle in His own words but gave a direct quotation. Satan is not rebuffed by clever phrases or theological arguments but his schemes are cut to pieces by the sword of the Spirit, which is the Word of God.

Week 4: The Fear of the Lord and a Godly Lifestyle

Opening Icebreaker

Although much is required of Christian leaders, all
believers are encouraged to be examples of living a holy
lifestyle. In fact the only Bible many people read is us
(2 Cor. 3:2–3; 1 Pet. 2:12, 3:1–2). Therefore we
should seek to 'purify ourselves from everything that
contaminates body and spirit, perfecting holiness out of
reverence for God' (2 Cor. 7:1).

Bible Readings

A number of references outside Nehemiah are given in
various notes to this session that you might like to read
as appropriate.

Aim of the Session

It is important to realise the effects of forsaking a
reverence for God. Here, the unity evident during the
early stages of the rebuilding project was shattered by
the exploitation of the poor by the rich. Their greed
precipitated a major crisis. Of all the tensions that arise
in society, the most difficult to resolve are those which
exist between the rich and the poor, the affluent and the
underprivileged. Paul referred to this issue (1 Cor. 11:17–
22), James wrote of the problem in his epistle (see James
2:1–13), and it continues to plague society to this very
day. God had decreed that to make provision for the poor,
the rich were to lend to them (Deut. 15:7–11) but without
charging interest (Exod. 22:25; Lev. 25:36). When we loose
our respect for God and His directions for living as laid
down in Scripture we expose ourselves to troubles.

When Scripture uses the term 'fear of the Lord' it is vital
to emphasise that this refers to respect, reverence and awe
for God, perhaps like meeting our Queen. We should not
be frightened of her but out of respect we would be on

our best behaviour and determined not to offend in any way. Some people are frightened of God because their concept of Him is as a vindictive judge who is determined to punish their every misdemeanour. Nothing could be further from the truth for Christ has already suffered our punishment that we might 'approach the throne of grace with confidence' (Heb. 4:16). Although Prince Charles shows respect for the Queen, she is still his 'mum'. So it is with us when we respect God but approach Him without fear because He is our loving Father.

The subject of holiness has been much debated amongst theologians. God forgives our sin and makes us holy, for ultimately Christ is our holiness (1 Cor. 1:30; Eph. 4:24). We are also clearly exhorted in Scripture to choose to live holy lives. The first is what God does in us. The second is what we allow God to do through us. One is a *position*, the other is a *process*. It is unthinkable that those who have received God's salvation should continue in a sin-filled lifestyle (Rom. 6:1–4). Rather, they should allow the life of Christ to be expressed through their own lives by showing love, forgiveness, purity, fairness, patience, compassion, faithfulness and so on. In this sense holiness would be defined not just by the wrong things we don't do, but also by the good fruit that the Holy Spirit produces in us (Gal. 5:22–23).

Nehemiah acknowledged his feelings of anger (5:6). He does not deny, excuse, minimise or dump his feelings on others. He keeps his anger under control and takes time to think through the issue (v.7), before deciding on a plan of action (vv.7–13). How different our lives would be if, whenever we became angry, we followed Nehemiah's example. First, acknowledge the anger. Second, choose not to allow it to get out of control. Third, carefully and prayerfully think through the best way of dealing with the situation (Eph. 4:26).

Week 5: Back to the Bible

Opening Icebreaker

A simple exercise to start the session but try to avoid either embarrassment or pride! If the group find this too easy try to list the books in order. You may need to write the names of all the books as a checklist.

Bible Readings

The additional New Testament readings emphasise the importance of not just hearing God's Word but also putting it into practice. James explains that if we read or listen to God's Word without putting it into practice we actually deceive ourselves.

Aim of the Session

The aim of this session is to highlight the principle of regular Bible reading and allowing its precepts to influence our attitudes and actions. The reading and explanation of God's Word took five or six hours during which time everyone listened attentively. Notice that it was not simply a matter of reading the Scriptures but of 'making it clear and giving the meaning so that the people could understand what was being read' (8:8).

We need to be careful that our Bible reading does not become an empty oppressive ritual but is a source of pleasure and spiritual strength. You might like to give time for people to honestly share their difficulties in regular Bible reading. Other people in the group could then explain how by changing the types of reading and using different Bible study aids we can always experience a freshness in our Bible readings. It can also help to use a more modern version such as *The Message* or New Living Translation.

The question about presenting Bible truths in our modern (non-book) culture is extremely challenging. Not too many years ago most children were taught Scripture in schools and at Sunday school. In our multi-cultural society this is often no longer the case and church attendance shows considerable decline. Books themselves compete with the latest technology and often lose out to computers or other leisure activities. Sometimes we can use this technology to our advantage. For example, Mel Gibson's film *The Passion of the Christ* has attracted vast audiences. There are many videos and computer DVDs of Christian teaching and Bible characters widely available in local Christian bookshops or through mail order. Some of these are particularly suitable for children or people with no previous Bible knowledge. The Alpha course has been replicated on a worldwide scale where people have a meal together and discuss a short talk on the Christian faith. Some churches or Christian groups are increasingly using drama – sometimes on the streets – in order to promote the message of the gospel. In an initiative reminiscent of the old passion plays for an illiterate population, one group in Surrey presents the play, *The Life of Christ*, in the grounds of a large estate where the audience at times become part of the action for scenes such as the feeding of the 5,000. The evangelist, J. John, has travelled the country presenting a series of talks on the Ten Commandments which he feels represent one of the few remaining points of cultural contact between the Church and the world. What could you and your church do?

Many years ago Mahatma Ghandi said to a group of missionaries, 'You Christians look after a document containing enough dynamite to blow all civilization to pieces, turn the world upside down and bring peace to a battle torn planet. But you treat it as though it is nothing more than a piece of literature'. The Bible is not just a book but *the* Book. It is God's Word to the world. Encourage the members of your group to read it, live it and spread its message far and wide.

Week 6: Principles of a Good Confession

Opening Icebreaker

A dictionary definition of confession includes the phrases 'to acknowledge', 'to admit' and 'to declare one's belief in'. Confession therefore not only involves acknowledgement of sins but also declaring our belief in God and His goodness. Confession is about speaking the truth. We speak the truth about our sins when we acknowledge them before God but we also confess when we speak the truth about the love of God and His salvation. Jesus made a 'good confession' before Pilate because He spoke the truth about Himself. The icebreaker is therefore meant to encourage people to see that confession is not just about sin but to speak out wonderful truths about God and His provision for us.

Bible Readings

It also may be helpful at the end of the study to read some of the verses referred to below about how God has blessed us. These could form the basis of a time of prayer when people confess the good things that God has done in their lives.

Aim of the Session

The aim of this session is largely explained in the icebreaker above. It is important that we confess our sins to God, but many Christians still seem to struggle with a guilt-ridden inferiority complex. God is not against us for our sin but for us against our sin. He loves us and it is good to remind ourselves of that by confessing scriptural truths such as, 'in [Christ] we have redemption through his blood, the forgiveness of sins' (Eph. 1:7), we are 'seated with [Christ] in the heavenly realms' (Eph. 2:6) and we 'are a chosen people, a royal priesthood, a holy nation, a people belonging to God' (1 Pet. 2:9). Although we should acknowledge our failures we should be even more conscious of the love and power of God at work in our lives. Jesus took our shame that we might be blameless with His righteousness before God (Isa. 53; Eph. 1:4; 2 Cor. 5:21). It is on that basis that we can boldly approach the throne of grace with confidence as a son or daughter of God (Heb. 4:16; Gal. 4:4–7).

We should be careful if we choose to confess our sins to another person and yet there can be a great power and release if we do. Often our confession is between us and God alone but James 5:16 says, 'confess your sins to each other'. This may involve saying 'I am sorry' to a person we have sinned against or confessing sins directly to God but with another person present. When the prodigal son returned home he confessed before his father that he had sinned 'against God and against you'. The son was clearly guilt stricken, 'I am no longer worthy to be called your son'. However the father was then able to assure him that he was forgiven and accepted as a loved member of the family (Luke 15:21–24). This serves to illustrate the second part of James 5:16, 'pray for each other so that you may be healed'.

One person has said: 'We have no light to illuminate the pathway of the future save that which falls over our shoulder from the past'. Reflecting on what God has done for us in the past enables us to have a clearer perspective on the present and the future. A biblical approach to history makes us neither wide-eyed optimists nor downhearted pessimists. We become devout realists, for we see God at work in all things and triumphing over everything including our failures and sins (Col. 2:13–15). As we contemplate the past and confess examples of God's goodness we draw hope and encouragement for the future.

Week 7: Covenant Commitment

Opening Icebreaker

The icebreaker is designed to encourage us to begin thinking about the nature of a covenant and will help answer the first of the discussion points. In a marriage ceremony, whether it is in a church or not, certain key elements are present. For example, there is an intermediary (minister or registrar), the parties to the covenant must be willing, they take a solemn oath, it is a binding agreement where the parties make promises to one another, it is written, signed, witnessed, includes terms of commitment and obligations, involves transfer of possessions, is legally recognised and joyfully celebrated (covenant meal). We can find many of these elements in the Nehemiah story and in our own commitment to Christ celebrated by taking communion.

Bible Readings

The readings have been extended to include passages that refer to the new covenant we have with God through Jesus so we can directly relate the Nehemiah story to our own experience.

Aim of the Session

It is vitally important for our spiritual wellbeing that we understand the nature of a covenant. As a binding agreement between God and His people, by making a covenant with us, God commits Himself to us in the strongest possible way. It is no vague or empty promise but a solemn undertaking to love, guide, protect and provide for us. A number of Christians find it difficult to believe that they are loved by God and are unsure of their salvation. They are often plagued by doubts and may be largely ineffective as a member of Christ's Body. When we are certain of God's love and commitment to us it produces within us a foundation of faith, security and confidence that is unshakeable. We know for sure that He will never leave us or forsake us (see Heb. 12:28, 13:5–6) and that no trouble, hardship, power or problem shall ever separate us from His love (Rom. 8:31–39). With that assurance we can stand firm against every accusation of the enemy who would seek to confuse and prevent us fulfilling the will of God in our own generation. Such confidence in God's love and our salvation is not a matter of pride or arrogance but of simply believing that what God's Word says about us is true (John 3:16, 10:28–29; Rom. 5:8).

There are different views about the Sabbath command-ment amongst various Christian traditions – from complete observance to almost total disregard. In our culture Sunday is now the second greatest trading day of the week. However, we should not be shaped by our culture but by God and His Word. Jesus pointed out that man's needs were more important than religious law (Mark 2:23–3:6), but we should always remember that man's greatest need is to set aside time to worship and relate to his Creator. We do need to establish priorities for we 'cannot serve both God and Money' (Matt. 6:24).

Nehemiah, like Christ, was a man of prayer who renounced a position of honour to serve God in uncomfortable, hostile conditions and overcame intense opposition in order to bring restoration and turn people back to God.

Covenants were often celebrated with a meal and time of rejoicing (eg, Gen. 25:26–31, 31:44–55). When covenant partners met again they would often remember and re-affirm their covenant commitment with another meal. Jesus introduced the new covenant during a meal and instructed us to take bread and wine in remembrance of Him and our new covenant with God through His blood. Depending on your church tradition, it may be appropriate to take communion in your group and celebrate our own covenant with God and all that it means.

Leader's Notes

National Distributors

UK: (and countries not listed below)
CWR, Waverley Abbey House, Waverley Lane, Farnham, Surrey GU9 8EP.
Tel: (01252) 784700 Outside UK (44) 1252 784700 Email: mail@cwr.org.uk

AUSTRALIA: KI Entertainment, Unit 21 317-321 Woodpark Road, Smithfield, New South Wales
2164. Tel: 1 800 850 777 Fax: 02 9604 3699 Email: sales@kientertainment.com.au

CANADA: David C Cook Distribution Canada, PO Box 98, 55 Woodslee Avenue, Paris,
Ontario N3L 3E5. Tel: 1800 263 2664 Email: swansons@cook.ca

GHANA: Challenge Enterprises of Ghana, PO Box 5723, Accra. Tel: (021) 222437/223249
Fax: (021) 226227 Email: ceg@africaonline.com.gh

HONG KONG: Cross Communications Ltd, 1/F, 562A Nathan Road, Kowloon.
Tel: 2780 1188 Fax: 2770 6229 Email: cross@crosshk.com

INDIA: Crystal Communications, 10-3-18/4/1, East Marredpalli, Secunderabad – 500026, Andhra
Pradesh. Tel/Fax: (040) 27737145 Email: crystal_edwj@rediffmail.com

KENYA: Keswick Books and Gifts Ltd, PO Box 10242-00400, Nairobi.
Tel: (254) 20 312639/3870125 Email: keswick@swiftkenya.com

MALAYSIA: Canaanland, No. 25 Jalan PJU 1A/41B, NZX Commercial Centre, Ara Jaya, 47301
Petaling Jaya, Selangor. Tel: (03) 7885 0540/1/2 Fax: (03) 7885 0545 Email: info@canaanland.com.my

Salvation Book Centre (M) Sdn Bhd, 23 Jalan SS 2/64, 47300 Petaling Jaya, Selangor.
Tel: (03) 78766411/78766797 Fax: (03) 78757066/78756360
Email: info@salvationbookcentre.com

NEW ZEALAND: KI Entertainment, Unit 21 317-321 Woodpark Road, Smithfield,
New South Wales 2164, Australia. Tel: 0 800 850 777 Fax: +612 9604 3699
Email: sales@kientertainment.com.au

NIGERIA: FBFM, Helen Baugh House, 96 St Finbarr's College Road, Akoka, Lagos.
Tel: (01) 7747429/4700218/825775/827264 Email: fbfm@hyperia.com

PHILIPPINES: OMF Literature Inc, 776 Boni Avenue, Mandaluyong City.
Tel: (02) 531 2183 Fax: (02) 531 1960 Email: gloadlaon@omflit.com

SINGAPORE: Alby Commercial Enterprises Pte Ltd, 95 Kallang Avenue #04-00, AIS Industrial
Building, 339420. Tel: (65) 629 27238 Fax: (65) 629 27235 Email: marketing@alby.com.sg

SOUTH AFRICA: Struik Christian Books, 80 MacKenzie Street, PO Box 1144, Cape Town 8000.
Tel: (021) 462 4360 Fax: (021) 461 3612 Email: info@struikchristianmedia.co.za

SRI LANKA: Christombu Publications (Pvt) Ltd, Bartleet House, 65 Braybrooke Place, Colombo 2.
Tel: (9411) 2421073/2447665 Email: dhanad@bartleet.com

USA: David C Cook Distribution Canada, PO Box 98, 55 Woodslee Avenue, Paris, Ontario N3L 3E5,
Canada. Tel: 1800 263 2664 Email: swansons@cook.ca

CWR is a Registered Charity – Number 294387
CWR is a Limited Company registered in England – Registration Number 1990308

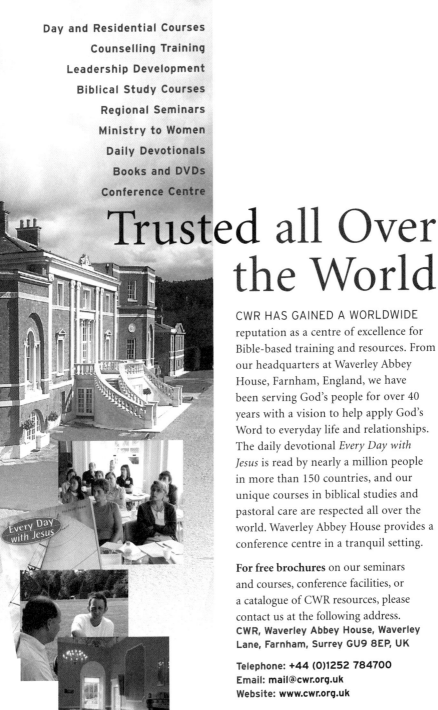

Day and Residential Courses
Counselling Training
Leadership Development
Biblical Study Courses
Regional Seminars
Ministry to Women
Daily Devotionals
Books and DVDs
Conference Centre

Trusted all Over the World

CWR HAS GAINED A WORLDWIDE reputation as a centre of excellence for Bible-based training and resources. From our headquarters at Waverley Abbey House, Farnham, England, we have been serving God's people for over 40 years with a vision to help apply God's Word to everyday life and relationships. The daily devotional *Every Day with Jesus* is read by nearly a million people in more than 150 countries, and our unique courses in biblical studies and pastoral care are respected all over the world. Waverley Abbey House provides a conference centre in a tranquil setting.

For free brochures on our seminars and courses, conference facilities, or a catalogue of CWR resources, please contact us at the following address. **CWR, Waverley Abbey House, Waverley Lane, Farnham, Surrey GU9 8EP, UK**

Telephone: **+44 (0)1252 784700**
Email: **mail@cwr.org.uk**
Website: **www.cwr.org.uk**

CWR Applying God's Word
to everyday life and relationships

Dramatic new resources

2 Corinthians: Restoring harmony
by Christine Platt

Paul's message went against the grain of the culture in Corinth, and even his humility was in stark contrast to Greco-Roman culture. Be challenged and inspired to endure suffering, seek reconciliation, pursue holiness and much more as you look at this moving letter which reveals Paul's heart as much as his doctrine. This thought-provoking, seven-week study guide is great for individual or small-group use.
ISBN: 978-1-85345-551-3

Isaiah 40-66: Prophet of restoration
by John Houghton

God is a God of new beginnings, a God of second chances who takes no pleasure in punishment. However, profound lessons must be learned if the same errors are to be avoided in the future. Understand Isaiah's powerful message for each of us, that God is a holy God who cannot ignore sin, but One who also displays amazing grace and mercy, and who longs to enjoy restored relationship with us. These seven inspiring and challenging studies are perfect for individual or small-group use.
ISBN: 978-1-85345-550-6

Also available in the bestselling
Cover to Cover Bible Study Series

1 Corinthians
Growing a Spirit-filled church
ISBN: 978-1-85345-374-8

1 Timothy
Healthy churches – effective Christians
ISBN: 978-1-85345-291-8

23rd Psalm
The Lord is my shepherd
ISBN: 978-1-85345-449-3

2 Timothy and Titus
Vital Christianity
ISBN: 978-1-85345-338-0

Ecclesiastes
Hard questions and spiritual answers
ISBN: 978-1-85345-371-7

Ephesians
Claiming your inheritance
ISBN: 978-1-85345-229-1

Esther
For such a time as this
ISBN: 978-1-85345-511-7

Fruit of the Spirit
Growing more like Jesus
ISBN: 978-1-85345-375-5

Genesis 1-11
Foundations of reality
ISBN: 978-1-85345-404-2

God's Rescue Plan
Finding God's fingerprints on human history
ISBN: 978-1-85345-294-9

Great Prayers of the Bible
Applying them to our lives today
ISBN: 978-1-85345-253-6

Hebrews
Jesus – simply the best
ISBN: 978-1-85345-337-3

Hosea
The love that never fails
ISBN: 978-1-85345-290-1

Isaiah 1-39
Prophet to the nations
ISBN: 978-1-85345-510-0

£3.99 each (plus p&p)
Price correct at time of printing

Cover to Cover Every Day
Gain deeper knowledge of the Bible

Each issue of these bimonthly daily Bible-reading notes gives
you insightful commentary on a book of the Old and New
Testaments with reflections on a psalm each weekend by
Philip Greenslade.

Enjoy contributions from two well-known authors every
two months, and over a five-year period you will be taken
through the entire Bible.

ISSN: 1744-0114
Only £2.49 each (plus p&p)
£13.80 for annual subscription (bimonthly, p&p included in UK)
£13.80 for annual email subscription
(available from www.cwr.org.uk/store)

Cover to Cover Complete
Read through the Bible chronologically

Take an exciting, year-long journey through the Bible, following events as they happened.

- See God's strategic plan of redemption unfold across the centuries
- Increase your confidence in the Bible as God's inspired message
- Come to know your heavenly Father in a deeper way

The full text of the flowing Holman Christian Standard Bible (HCSB) provides an exhilarating reading experience and is augmented by our beautiful:

- Illustrations
- Maps
- Charts
- Diagrams
- Timeline

And key Scripture verses and devotional thoughts make each day's reading more meaningful.

ISBN: 978-1-85345-433-2
Only £19.99 (plus p&p)

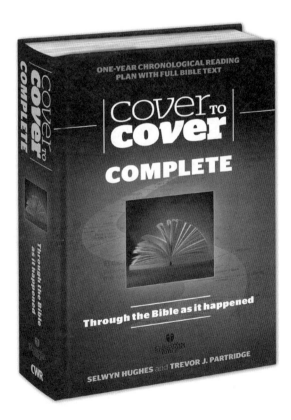